Christmas Storybook

Bible stories, activities, and a devotion

for **YoungReaders**™

Illustrated by Jenifer Schneider

STANDARD PUBLISHING
Cincinnati, Ohio

The Standard Publishing Company, Cincinnati, Ohio. A division of Standex International Corporation
© 1996 The Standard Publishing Company. All rights reserved. Designed by Coleen Davis
Printed in the United States of America. ISBN 0-7847-0543-7

Mary Meets an Angel

from Luke 1

Young Mary of Nazareth was engaged to marry Joseph.

But before the wedding day, the angel Gabriel came.
"Hello, Mary," said the angel. "The Lord is with you."

What does this mean? wondered Mary.

"Don't be afraid," the angel said. "You have found favor with God."

Gabriel had big news for Mary.
"You are going to have
a baby boy," he said.
"You will name him Jesus.
He will be great,
and his kingdom will never end."
"How can this be?" asked Mary.
"I don't have a husband."

"God's Holy Spirit will come
upon you," said the angel.
"That is why the baby
will be called the Son of God.
And your cousin Elizabeth
is having a child,
even though she is old.
Nothing is impossible with God."

"I have always loved God," Mary said quietly.
"And I will be his servant. Let everything happen just as you have said." Then the angel left as quickly as he had appeared.

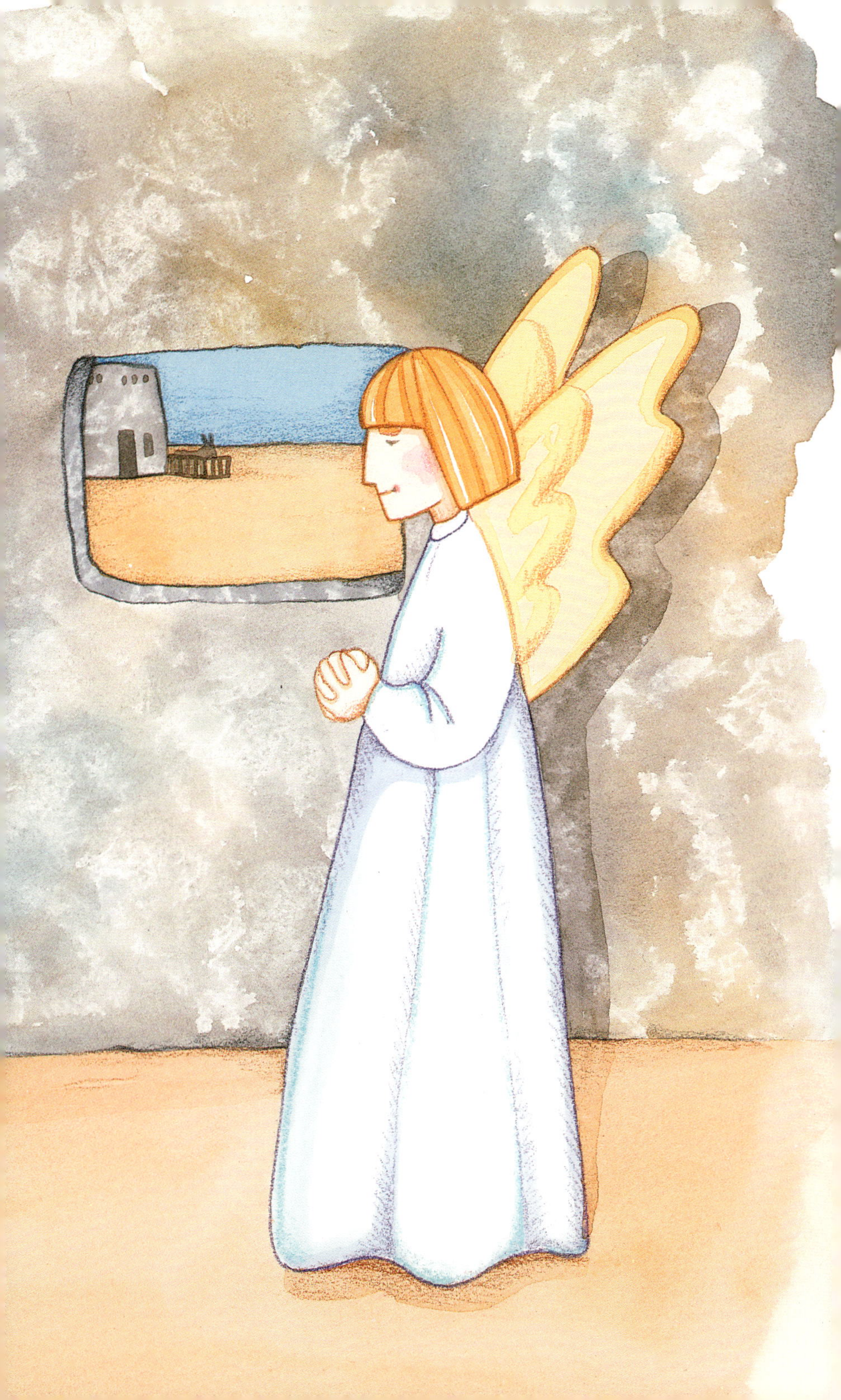

One Night in Bethlehem
from Luke 2

"The king wants to know how many people are in his kingdom," Joseph told Mary. "We must go to my hometown and be counted."

Mary patted her large middle. "Bethlehem is far away, Joseph," she sighed. "And the baby is due any day now."

"Please don't worry,"

Joseph told Mary.

"God will watch over us."

The trip to Bethlehem
was long and dusty.
And Bethlehem was crowded.
Joseph tried to find a room
where they could stay.
"Sorry," said the innkeeper.
"Every room here is full."

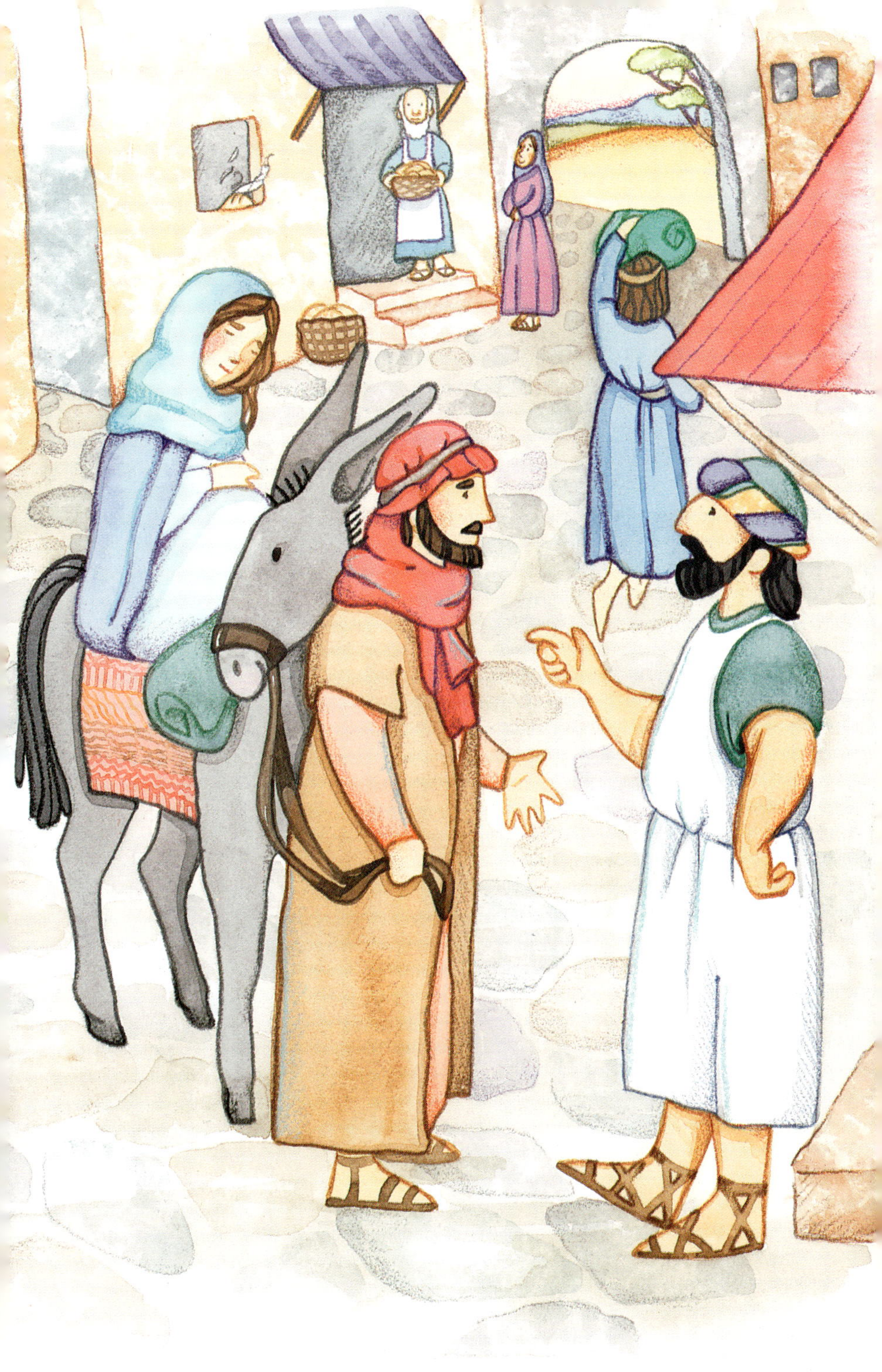

But Mary and Joseph
found a warm, clean stable.
And there Mary's baby was born.
The baby was a boy, Jesus,
just as God's angel had said!

Mary wrapped her newborn baby
in cloths to keep him warm.
Tenderly she laid him
in his first bed —
a simple feeding box
under the stars,
one night in Bethlehem.

Good News of Great Joy

from Luke 2

On the hills near Bethlehem, shepherds watched their sheep. Suddenly the night was bright! And standing near the shepherds was an angel of the Lord.

The shepherds were afraid!
But the angel said,
"Calm down, for I have come
with good news of great joy!
Today in Bethlehem
a Savior has been born to you.
Christ the Lord has come!"

"You may go to see him,"
the angel told the shepherds.
"This will be a sign for you.
You will find the baby
wrapped in cloths
and lying in a feeding box."

Then there were angels
all around,
praising God and saying,
"Glory to God in the highest!
And peace to his people
on earth!"

When the angels were gone,
the shepherds said,
"Let's go to Bethlehem!"
They hurried into town
and found Mary and Joseph
and the baby, just as the angel
had said.

Then the shepherds went back
to their sheep,
praising God all the way.

Follow That Star!

from Matthew 2

Wise men from the east came to Jerusalem.
"Where is the child who was born king of the Jews?" they asked.
"We saw his star in the east.
We have come to worship him."

King Herod was angry.
He wanted to be the only king!
He called the Jewish leaders.
"Tell me where the Christ
will be born," he said.
"In Bethlehem," they told him,
"just as the prophet wrote."

"Go to Bethlehem,"

Herod told the wise men.

"Look for the child there.

When you find him,

come and tell me.

I want to worship him, too."

But King Herod was lying.

He did not want

to worship the baby.

He wanted to have him killed.

The wise men left for Bethlehem.

"Look!" they said.

"There is the star again."

They followed the star
until it stopped
right over the house
where Jesus was.

The wise men went inside.

They saw Jesus

with Mary, his mother.

They bowed down

to worship him

and gave him precious gifts.

That night in a dream,
God sent a warning
to the wise men.
"Do not go back
to King Herod," God said.
So the wise men went home
by a different road.

Busy Bethlehem

Help Mary and Joseph find their way through the crowd to the inn.

What's Wrong?

Jesus was born in a stable in Bethlehem. How many things can you find wrong with this picture?

Answer: 6

Look at That Star!

What are your favorite
Christmas decorations?
Do you put up lights
on your house?
Maybe you have a star
for the top of your tree.

There was a very special star
one night long ago.
The star was God's sign
that Jesus was born.
The star led the wise men to Jesus.
They worshiped Jesus
and gave him gifts.

What can we give to Jesus?
We can give him our love.
We can give him our time.
We can give him our songs
and the kind things
we do for others.
When you see star decorations
this Christmas,
remember the wise men.
Think of what you can give
to Jesus!

A Verse to Learn

☆ They gave him treasures of gold,
frankincense, and myrrh.
Matthew 2:11

A Story to Read

☆ "Follow That Star!"
on page 250 of *The Young Reader's Bible,*
or
☆ Matthew 2:1-12

Something to Pray

☆ Dear God, I want to give to Jesus this
Christmas. Help me think of a way.

Something to Do

☆ Make a star for your tree. Paint it yellow.
While the paint is wet, sprinkle on
a little salt or glitter to make it sparkle.

There are many other *Young Readers* products for you and your children to enjoy!

Look for these at your favorite Christian bookstore.

The Young Reader's Bible (24-03950). Kids 5 to 8 who are reading on their own will feel right at home with this age-appropriate Bible. From Genesis to Revelation, all 70 stories are short enough to finish in one sitting. It's the perfect way to start a child on a lifetime of personal Bible reading. Features include maps of Bible lands, time line, illustrated Bible who's who, "How Did We Get the Bible?" and a glossary.

The Young Reader's Bible on Cassette (24-23950). Capture all the fun and excitement of The Young Reader's Bible with this 110-minute cassette! Narrated by young children, all 70 stories from the original Young Reader's Bible are included with background music and sound effects that help capture a young child's imagination. Use the cassette as a great read-along companion to The Young Reader's Bible or as a stand-alone audio book. Great for traveling and bedtime, too!

Devotions for Young Readers (24-02756). One of the greatest things a child can learn is the importance of spending time alone with God. Now children will look forward to their own quiet time with Devotions for Young Readers. This collection of 52 devotions features the same artwork and easy-to-read format as the best-selling Young Reader's Bible. Each devotion contains a passage of Scripture, a corresponding Young Reader's Bible story, and activities that encourage children to put each lesson into action.

The Young Reader's Bible Double Fun Pads. These compact activity books are really two books in one—just flip them over to start a whole new set of fun activities. And after kids complete an activity, they can color in the page. A fun and challenging way to learn about the Bible. Great for traveling, too!
    Double Fun Pad #1 (23-22107)
    Double Fun Pad #2 (23-22108)